AF226568

SOME DADS SUCK WAY MORE THAN YOU

22 Wild Examples of Why You're a Great Dad

Karen E. Mueller, DVM

Illustrated by Jennifer Mills

K. Mueller Publishing

ISBN 978-1-971218-00-7 Paperback

ISBN 978-1-971218-01-4 Hardback

Cover Design by Wild Bloom Publishing.

First Edition 2025.

Printed in the United States of America.

K. Mueller Publishing

Bellingham, WA, USA

For every dad who keeps showing up with love —
even when it's anything but easy.

INTRODUCTION

Being a dad is awesome.
But let's be honest—
moms usually get most of the credit.
Even if you're the one doing all (and I mean all) the heavy lifting—literally—your baby's first word is still more likely to be "Mommy." Or "cookie." Or "poopy."
Totally unfair, right?

And sure, sometimes you might feel like you're falling short. Like, maybe you kind of suck at this whole dad thing.
But here's the truth: you don't.
Not even close.

This book will prove it—
by showing you 22 dads out there
who suck way more
than you ever could.

SAND GOBY

Sand goby dads are great protectors—until the water gets low on oxygen.

Then the kids don't look like babies anymore. They start looking like lunch.

That's super sucky.
You sure don't suck like that.

GIANT WATER BUG

Giant water bug moms glue their eggs onto dad's back.

But if he's carrying too many, the eggs can suffocate— or he turns into a live buffet for predators.

That's pretty sucky.
That sucks way worse than you.

DARWIN'S FROG

Darwin's frog dads really put their money where their mouth is.

They withhold their babies in their vocal sacs while they develop— then sometimes swallow the whole investment instead of letting it grow.

That's outrageously sucky. You'd never suck that selfishly.

CUCKOO CATFISH

Cuckoo catfish dads are the masters of the swap.

They trick another fish into raising their kids—then their babies eat the foster sibs.

That's one sucky setup—a pretty sucky welcome to the world.

EASTERN BLUEBIRD

Eastern bluebird dads sometimes bail on the family.

They'll find a new mate, then drive off the old one—*and the kids!*

That's some seriously sucky supervision.

Bluebird dads suck way more than you.

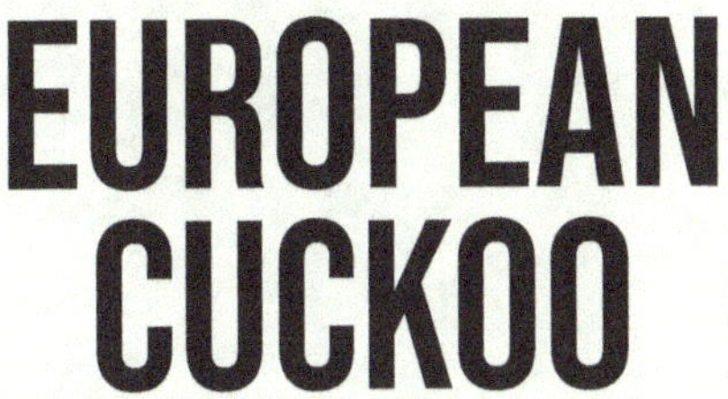

EUROPEAN CUCKOO

European cuckoo dads are world-class slackers.

Their mates lay eggs in other birds' nests, and the hosts end up raising the chicks.

That’s parenting by outsourcing—at its suckiest.

You’d never suck like that.

CARDINALFISH

Cardinalfish dads guard their eggs by holding them in their mouths.

But sometimes they just can't resist— and those babies go straight down the hatch.

That's spectacularly sucky. You just can't suck like that.

PIPEFISH

Pipefish dads carry the babies in their brood pouch, like they're pregnant.

But if the female wasn't attractive enough, he absorbs those embryos back into himself.

Seriously?!

That's a sucky step you'd never take— a real textbook case of suck.

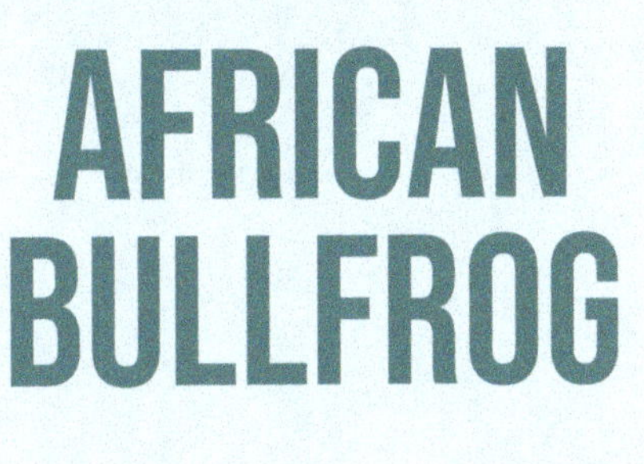

AFRICAN BULLFROG

African bullfrog dads guard their tadpoles like tough bodyguards.

But if there isn't enough food around, their tadpoles become the meals.

That's amazingly sucky. You couldn't possibly suck like that.

Greater rhea dads hatch and raise dozens of chicks.

But when a chick is weak, dads may turn on them instead.

That's a really sucky parenting choice.

You'd never suck like a Rhea.

RED-FOOTED BOOBY

Red-footed booby dads play favorites.

The weaker chick gets shoved out of the nest, and dad doesn't lift a wing.

With a name like Booby, you'd think they're dumb, not heartless.

That's a whole new level of suck.

SMALL BLUEGILL SUNFISH

Small bluegill sunfish dads are tricksters.

They dress up like females, slip in to fertilize another nest, then let the other guy raise their kids.

That's undercover sucky. You'd never sink to that kind of suck.

KOMODO DRAGON

Komodo dragon dads don't bother with parenting.

In their world, children are ignored.

But if they're noticed, they're swallowed.

That's as sucky as it gets. You're miles ahead of that kind of suck.

BLACK EAGLE

Black eagle dads drop off the food—
then watch from the sidelines while one chick attacks the other.

That's taking suck to new heights.

You couldn't suck like that if you tried.

BEARDED DRAGON

Bearded dragon dads nail the dance moves—then vanish when the babies arrive.

That’s a sucky plan if there ever was one.

You don't suck anywhere near that bad.

STICKLEBACK FISH

Stickleback dads work hard at first—building nests and fanning eggs.

But when conditions get tough, the babies become dinner.

That's a textbook case of suck—
a truly sucky splash.

PRAYING MANTIS

Praying mantis dads don't even get the chance to be bad parents.

They end up as dinner before the kids are born.

That's a world-class kind of suck.

You'd never suck that badly.

When a black widow dad
meets “the one,”
it’s his first chance at love—
and his last dance—
all in the same night.

Some dates really suck the
life out of you.

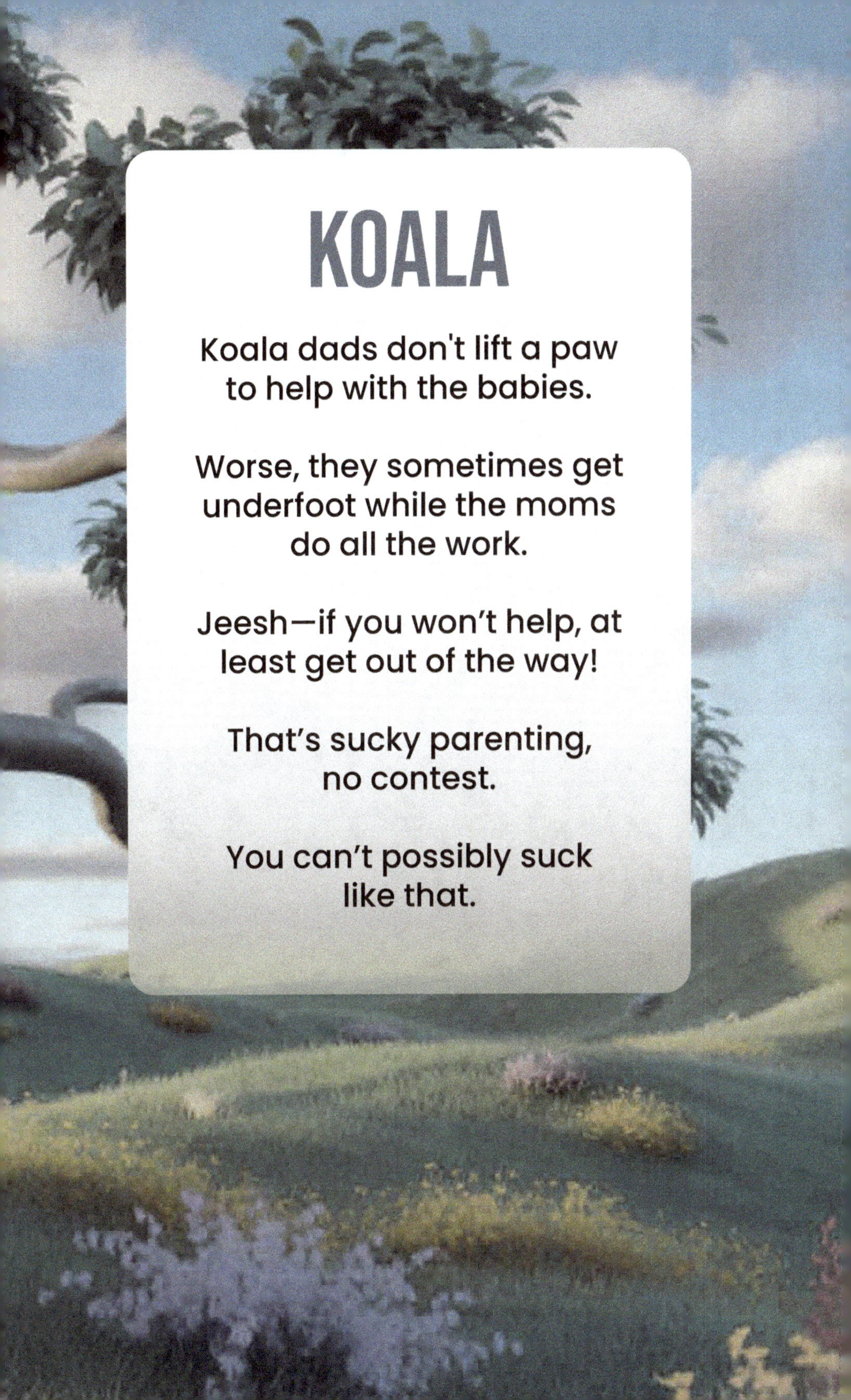

KOALA

Koala dads don't lift a paw to help with the babies.

Worse, they sometimes get underfoot while the moms do all the work.

Jeesh—if you won't help, at least get out of the way!

That's sucky parenting, no contest.

You can't possibly suck like that.

HOUSE SPARROW

House sparrow dads fight off rivals with gusto.

Too bad they forget to bring food home to their kids.

That's one sucky slip you'll never make.

Good thing you don't suck like that.

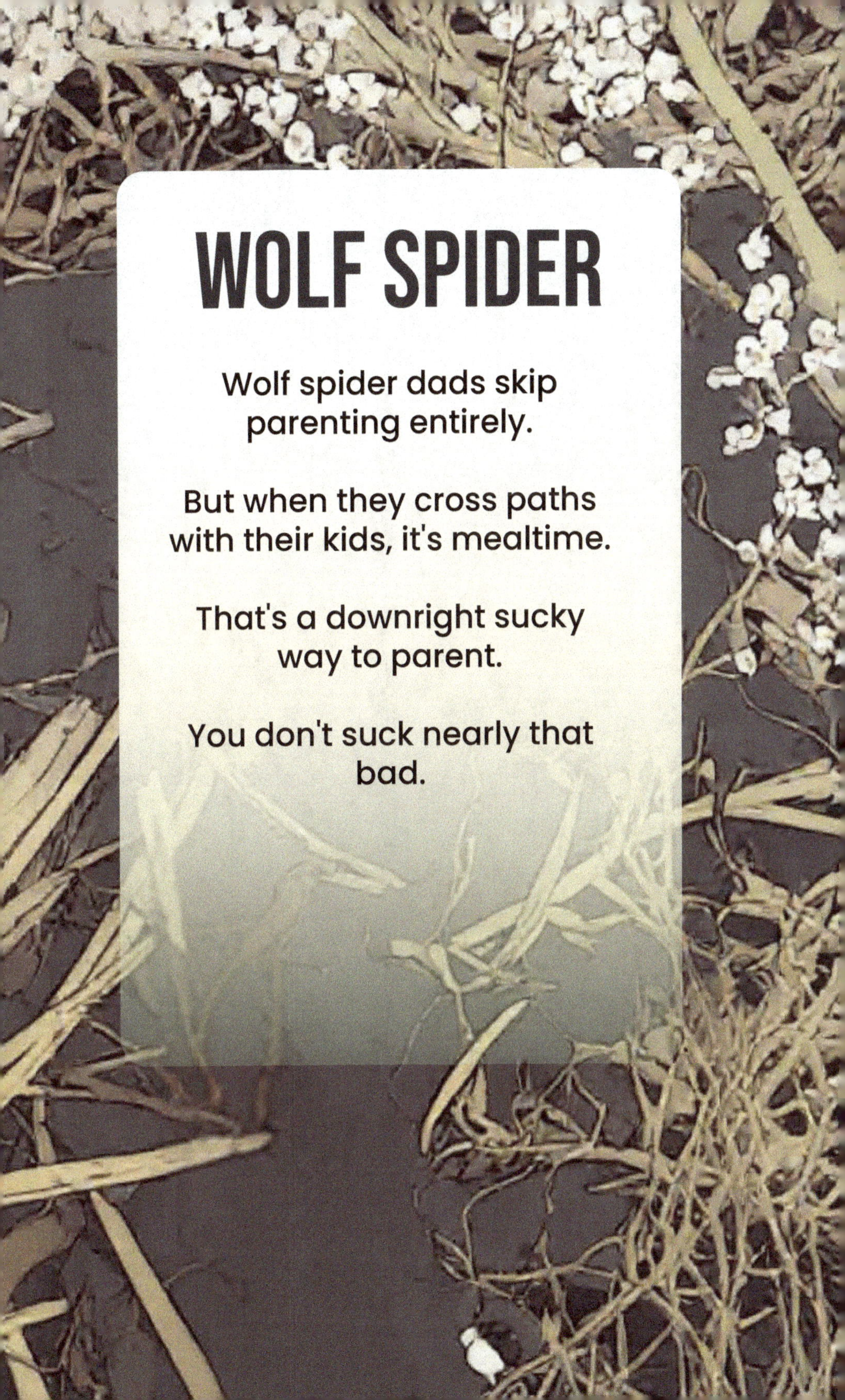

WOLF SPIDER

Wolf spider dads skip parenting entirely.

But when they cross paths with their kids, it's mealtime.

That's a downright sucky way to parent.

You don't suck nearly that bad.

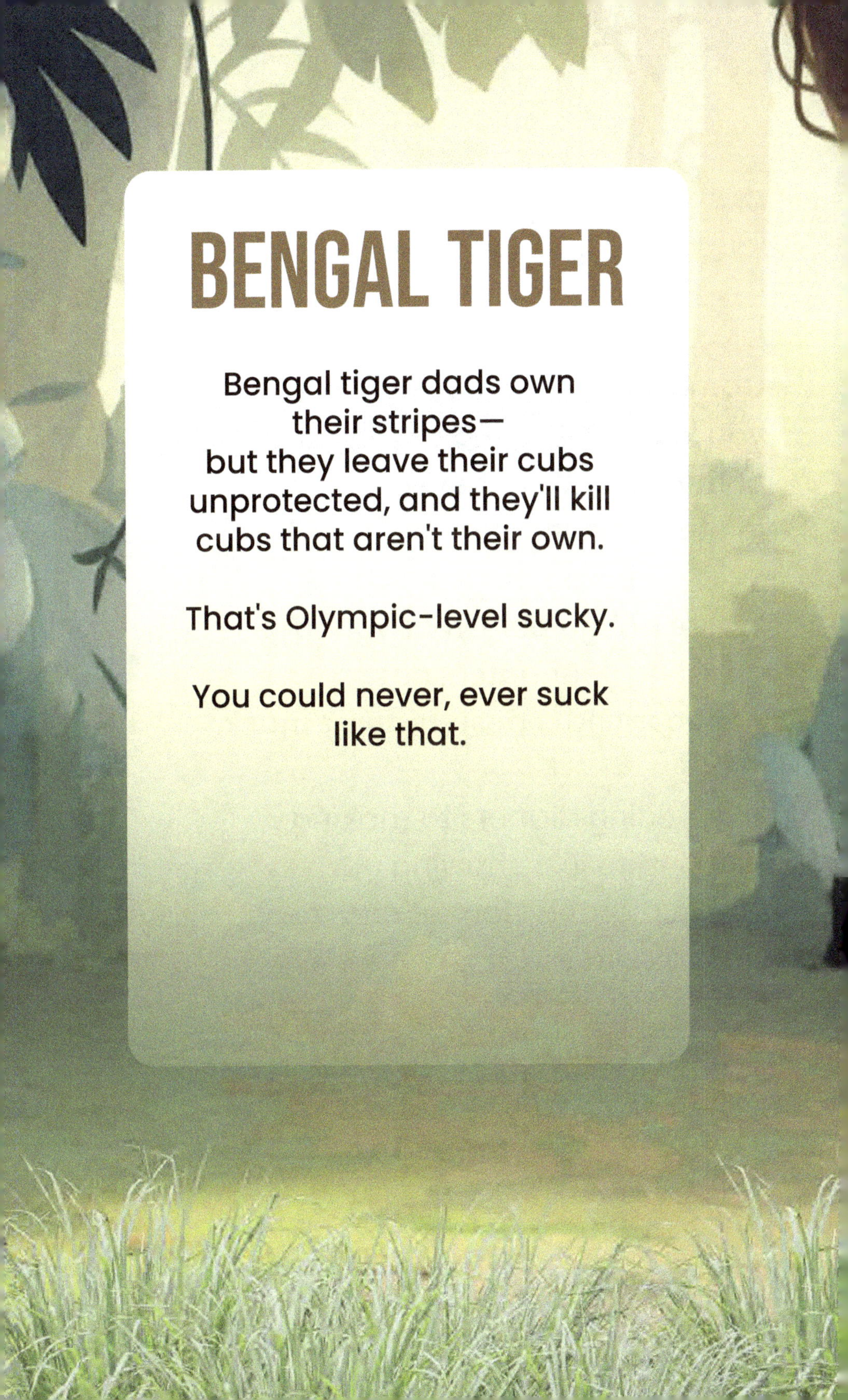

BENGAL TIGER

Bengal tiger dads own
their stripes—
but they leave their cubs
unprotected, and they'll kill
cubs that aren't their own.

That's Olympic-level sucky.

You could never, ever suck
like that.

CONCLUSION

So now you have it.
Compared to the dads you've just met,
you knock fathering so far out
of the park, it's not even
in the same league.

You're not gulping your young,
ghosting your hatchlings,
or becoming a post-mating snack.

From doing diapers to making
lunches, to just showing up,
you're a grand slam of dad-ness
(just ask your kids).

You don't suck at being a dad—
you're doing better than you know.

FROM DEADBEATS TO DARWIN

THE EVOLUTIONARY LOGIC OF LAZY FATHERHOOD

You've just met some of the world's most questionable fathers—but in nature, even the worst parenting has a purpose. This section looks at the curious ways fatherhood evolved across species, from the all-in dads who guard the nest to the ones who vanish (or get eaten) right after the first date. In the wild, though, what looks like lousy parenting can actually be a successful strategy.

But be reassured: Compared to them, your human way of being a dad already counts as a victory.

SAND GOBY

(POMATOSCHISTUS MINUTUS)

Sand Goby dads are usually quite devoted. They guard their nests diligently and even fan their eggs to keep them well oxygenated. This fanning not only keeps the water moving but also helps remove waste and prevent fungal growth. It's like being a stay-at-home dad with a leaf blower.

But if oxygen levels drop or resources run low, the goby changes tactics. He starts eating some of his eggs—typically the least likely to survive. From an evolutionary standpoint, this brutal efficiency makes sense: sacrificing a few conserves energy and oxygen for the rest. Think of it as starting the empty nest phase... just a little ahead of schedule.

GIANT WATER BUG

(BELOSTOMATIDAE)

Fatherhood gets intense for Giant Water Bugs. After mating, the female glues a cluster of eggs onto the male's back, turning him into a walking nursery. He spends the next week or two protecting and oxygenating the eggs by doing push-ups in the water to keep fresh flow circulating. It's one of the more hands-on cases of insect paternity in the animal kingdom.

But the system has a flaw: too many eggs can weigh the male down, making it harder for him to breathe or avoid predators. And unlike some animals, he doesn't have the option to scrape them off. If the situation goes south, he's stuck—literally—with a potentially fatal load. Insect fatherhood: it's all fun and games until you can't surface for air.

DARWIN'S FROG

(RHINODERMA DARWINII)

Darwin's Frog takes "close parenting" to a whole new level. After the female lays her eggs, the male waits for them to develop—then slurps them into his vocal sac. The tadpoles continue to grow there, safe from predators and environmental dangers—though there's always the chance he might eat a few by accident… or on purpose.

This bizarre babysitting gig actually serves a brilliant evolutionary function. By carrying the developing young inside his body, the father shields them from the hazards of the outside world —no drying puddles, no lurking predators. It's unconventional but pretty effective, if you don't mind your kids living in your throat.

CUCKOO CATFISH

(SYNODONTIS MULTIPUNCTATUS)

Cuckoo Catfish are the aquatic con artists of Lake Tanganyika. These fish sneak their eggs into the mouths of unsuspecting mouthbrooding cichlids—fish that carry their own eggs and fry in their mouths for protection. The catfish time it perfectly, laying their eggs during a cichlid's spawn so they get scooped up in the confusion.

It doesn't stop at freeloading. Once inside the host's mouth, the catfish hatch faster than the cichlid fry and may even eat their foster siblings. It's ruthless but remarkably effective—no parenting required, just perfect timing and zero shame. In the world of bad dads, that's about as good as it gets.

EASTERN BLUEBIRD

(SIALIA SIALIS)

Eastern Bluebird fathers usually pitch in to feed the chicks and guard the nest—but sometimes, things take a sharp left turn. If a male finds a new mate while his previous brood is still in the nest, he may drive off the old female and her young to start fresh. The chicks are left to fend for themselves—or not.

It might sound heartless, but in the wild, it can make reproductive sense. If a male thinks a new partner offers better odds of passing on his genes, he'll choose the future over the present. When it comes to bluebird dads, commitment only lasts until the next nest.

EUROPEAN CUCKOO

(CUCULUS CANORUS)

European Cuckoos are the classic freeloaders of the bird world. After mating with multiple males, the female lays her eggs in the nests of other birds—usually smaller, more nurturing species like warblers or pipits. The unsuspecting hosts end up raising a chick that's larger than their own and far more demanding.

This parenting strategy—called brood parasitism—is an evolutionary shortcut. Instead of investing energy in building nests or feeding chicks, cuckoos focus on laying as many eggs as possible in as many nests as possible. It's quantity over quality—and for cuckoo parents, outsourcing is the ultimate parenting plan.

CARDINAL FISH

(APOGON IMBERBIS)

Cardinalfish are mouthbrooders, meaning the dads carry fertilized eggs in their mouths to keep them safe until they hatch. It's a big commitment—no eating, no talking, and definitely no dad snacks when your mouth is full of developing offspring.

But if the male gets too hungry or stressed, he might quietly eat the whole brood. It's not ideal, but in evolutionary terms, staying alive to spawn another day may matter more than risking everything for one batch of eggs. No one said fatherhood was easy to swallow.

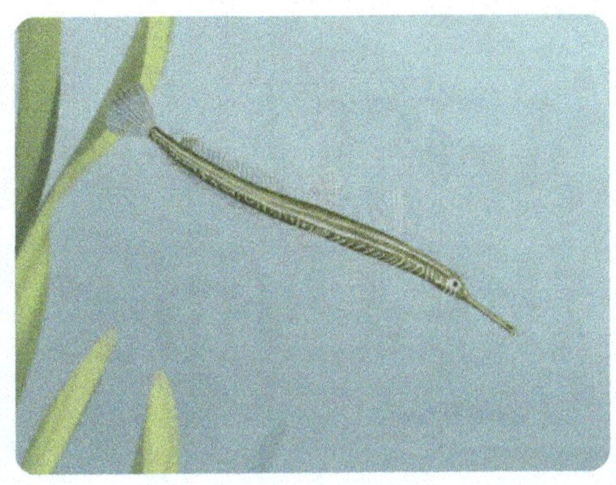

PIPEFISH

(SYNGNATHUS TYPHLE)

Pipefish dads are seahorse relatives, and like seahorses, the males carry the young. Females deposit fertilized eggs into a special brood pouch on the male's body, where the embryos develop. But not all embryos get equal treatment. Males sometimes "reabsorb" eggs from less desirable mates—essentially turning them into a quick protein snack.

It's a strategy rooted in mate choice. If a male is courted by multiple females, he may invest only in the offspring of the healthiest or most attractive ones. It's not cold-hearted; just calorie-smart parenting in a crowded ocean dating pool. Who needs meal prep when you can recycle?

AFRICAN BULLFROG

(PYXICEPHALUS ADSPERSUS)

African Bullfrog dads put in serious effort—at least at first. They fiercely guard their wriggling tadpoles and will even dig channels to help them escape drying puddles. But when food runs low, things can take a dark turn: Dad may end up eating some of the tadpoles himself.

It's a gruesome twist, but also a survival strategy. In a shrinking habitat, thinning the crowd may give a few strong tadpoles a better shot at adulthood. And those extra calories might keep Dad alive long enough to help the rest make it to the froglet stage. For bullfrog dads, tough love sometimes means tadpole takeout.

GREATER RHEA

(RHEA AMERICANA)

Greater Rhea males are overachievers at first glance: they build the nests, incubate the eggs, and care for up to 30 chicks from multiple females. But there's a darker side to their efficiency—if a chick is weak or struggling, the male might abandon it or even peck it to death.

It might seem brutal, but it's a classic case of triage parenting. By focusing on the strongest chicks, the male improves the odds that at least some will survive to adulthood. In the wild, resources are limited and time is short. When you're raising 30 chicks, natural selection starts to look like good parenting.

RED-FOOTED BOOBY

(SULA SULA)

Red-footed Boobies typically lay two eggs, but only one chick usually survives. Why? Because the stronger chick often shoves the weaker one out of the nest—and the parents don't intervene. It's called siblicide, and in this family dynamic, it's more of a shrug than a tragedy.

From an evolutionary perspective, it makes sense. Raising one strong chick is better than losing both if food is scarce. The second egg is just an insurance policy in case the first one fails. Brutal? Absolutely. Efficient? Without question. When you're a booby chick, sharing isn't part of the lesson plan.

SMALL BLUEGILL SUNFISH

(LEPOMIS MACROCHIRUS)

Among Bluegill Sunfish, not all males are created equal. Some are nest-builders and caregivers, diligently guarding eggs and fry. But others—the so-called "sneaker males"—pretend to be females to slip in and fertilize eggs in another male's nest. The result? One guy does all the work raising a batch of kids that may not even be his.

It's a sly strategy that spreads genes without investing in real estate or childcare. For the hardworking dads, it's a genetic gamble—and they'll never even know they lost. For the sneaker males, it's evolution's version of a free ride.

KOMODO DRAGON

(VARANUS KOMODOENSIS)

Komodo Dragons don't do diaper duty—or any parental duty, really. After laying eggs, female Komodos cover them with soil and leaves, then head off without a second glance. Hatchlings are left to fend for themselves—and to avoid adults, including their own dads—because adult Komodos aren't above snacking on the young.

It might sound extreme, but for a solitary predator in a harsh environment, it's a practical trade-off. The hatchlings that make it are really fast and good at climbing trees—because in a Komodo household, you wouldn't want to be caught dead at storytime.

BLACK EAGLE

(ICTINAETUS MALAIENSIS)

Black Eagles typically raise only one chick, even though they often lay two eggs. When both chicks hatch, the older or stronger one usually attacks and kills the other. The parents don't intervene—they just keep feeding the winner.

It's a ruthless form of sibling rivalry—classic siblicide—that ensures the strongest chick survives, especially when food is scarce. For Black Eagles, sibling rivalry isn't a phase—it's a business plan.

BEARDED DRAGON

(POGONA VITTICEPS)

Male Bearded Dragons put on quite a fancy courtship show—head bobs, arm waves, and pushups galore. But once the mating display is over, so is their involvement. They don't stick around to guard eggs, protect hatchlings, or even offer lizard snacks.

This hands-off approach is common in reptiles, especially species whose babies are independent from birth. For Bearded Dragons, the goal is to pass on genes and move along. They've already mastered push-ups and posing. Diaper duty isn't part of the routine.

STICKLEBACK FISH

(GASTEROSTEUS ACULEATUS)

Male Sticklebacks are meticulous nest builders and attentive dads—at first. They lure females to lay eggs in their carefully crafted nests, then fertilize and guard the clutch, fanning water over the eggs to keep them oxygenated. But if oxygen levels drop or stress runs high, these devoted dads can flip from protector to predator—and eat their own offspring.

It sounds shocking, but the logic is purely evolutionary. When conditions deteriorate, the odds of survival plummet. By consuming the clutch, the male recoups valuable energy for future mating opportunities. It's not heartless—it's just a life insurance payout—with Dad as the beneficiary.

PRAYING MANTIS

(MANTIS RELIGIOSA)

Male Praying Mantises face a deadly courtship. Females will often eat the male during or after mating. That leaves no chance for fatherhood—he's already a high-protein snack by the time the eggs are laid.

Still, the sacrifice may serve a purpose. Cannibalized males can boost the female's nutrition, leading to healthier offspring. It's not exactly father-son bonding; rather, a gruesome kind of dedication to the next generation. Parenting: it's what's for dinner.

BLACK WIDOW SPIDER

(LATRODECTUS MACTANS)

Male Black Widows have it rough from the start. They risk their lives just getting close enough to mate, tiptoeing around females that are larger, faster, and armed with far more venom. Courtship is cautious—one wrong move, and he's dinner instead of a date.

Even if mating goes well, it usually ends the same way: with the male consumed. With no chance of paternal care, his entire evolutionary job is to find a mate, pass on his genes, and probably become a protein-packed meal. Best-case scenario: a fatal form of family planning.

KOALA

(PHASCOLARCTOS CINEREUS)

Male Koalas are mostly absent when it comes to child-rearing. They don't help raise joeys and sometimes even interfere with mothers trying to care for their young. Their job ends with mating—after that, it's back to napping, bellowing, and eating eucalyptus while avoiding childcare entirely.

Koala dads just weren't built for nurturing—they were built for chill. Their energy goes into maintaining territory and attracting mates, not rocking joeys to sleep. Koala dads might be endangered, but their parenting skills were extinct to begin with.

HOUSE SPARROW

(PASSER DOMESTICUS)

Male House Sparrows are territorial and fiercely protective of their mates. Sometimes they spend so much energy chasing off rivals and guarding their "rights" to their partners that they forget to feed the chicks. Priorities? Questionable. Parental instincts? Lame.

But this behavior isn't just bravado. In the wild, ensuring paternity can be just as important as caring for offspring. By focusing on guarding mates, sparrow dads increase the odds that the chicks they feed are really their own. End of the day: everyone's hungry, but at least they're his.

WOLF SPIDER

(HOGNA CAROLINENSIS)

Male Wolf Spiders don't stick around to parent at all, leaving the moms to do all the heavy lifting—or in this case, the heavy carrying. Female wolf spiders are famously devoted, toting their egg sacs everywhere and letting their spiderlings ride on their backs after hatching. But dad? He's long gone, doing his part during mating and skittering off into the underbrush. If he ever does cross paths with his own offspring, he probably won't recognize them—or worse, he might just eat them.

As grim as that sounds, it makes a certain kind of sense in the spider world. Most male spiders aren't built for long-term commitment; their small size and short lives leave them unsuited for childcare. And hanging around after mating usually means becoming a snack for mom. Call it a deadbeat move—or just staying off the menu.

BENGAL TIGER

(PANTHERA TIGRIS TIGRIS)

Male Bengal Tigers are undeniably majestic—powerful, solitary, and territorial. But fatherhood? That's not high on their priority list. A male tiger will often kill cubs that aren't his own, especially after taking over a new territory. And while he may sire a litter or two, he's not winning any Father of the Year awards. He doesn't stick around to provide food, shelter, or protection. That's all left to the mother, who raises the cubs alone in the dense jungle, teaching them to hunt and survive.

Why such a brutal approach? From a biological standpoint, infanticide increases the chances that the female will come back into heat sooner—giving the male a chance to pass on his genes. Of course, reproduction isn't the same as parenting—fatherhood was never a tiger's strong suit. It's not personal—it's a real jungle out there.

FINAL THOUGHTS:

Survival of the Barely Involved

Look, parenting in the wild is no walk in the savannah. These animals may seem like they've epically failed Fatherhood 101. Still, in their own rugged ecosystems, they're just doing what works—even if it means freeloading, vanishing, or letting the kids fend for themselves. Nature is weird, resourceful, and brutally efficient. But it's hard not to laugh (or cringe) at how low the bar can get sometimes.

You, on the other hand, have shown up for the real stuff—diapers, fevers, late-night worries, school plays, meltdown negotiations, and all the tiny crises that pop up between breakfast and bedtime. Compared to these wild dads, you're basically a superhero with snacks. Not only have you survived being a dad—you've rocked it.

And don't underestimate how much it matters that you keep showing up. Even when you're tired, wired, and stretched thinner than floss, you're still there—fixing things, cheering them on, and doing the heavy lifting—both emotional and literal. Whether you're guiding your kids through big feelings, coaching from the sidelines, or just trying to keep everyone fed and functioning, you're doing something extraordinary. Being present isn't flashy, but it's powerful. And you do it day after day.

So go ahead—give yourself a well-earned fist bump. Being a dad isn't about perfection; it's about effort, patience, humor, and heart. And you've brought all of that, even on the days that felt like more than one dad could possibly juggle. You've not only survived fatherhood—you've owned it.

Way to go, Dad!

KAREN E. MUELLER, DVM

(AUTHOR)

Karen E. Mueller, DVM was born and raised in the Pacific Northwest, where a lifelong love of animals inspired both her veterinary career and her curiosity about the natural world. A veterinarian, educator, author, and mom of two, Dr. Mueller has spent her professional life caring for animals while also writing books that connect science with storytelling.

As the creator of the "Sucks Series," she blends real natural history with laugh-out-loud humor to celebrate imperfect parents everywhere. With titles like *Some Moms Suck Way More Than You* and Some *Dads Suck Way More Than You*—and more on the way —her books remind readers that perfection is overrated, presence matters most, and even the animal kingdom has its share of spectacular parenting fails.

Dr. Mueller is passionate about making science approachable, whether she's writing about cryptids, teaching animal behavior, or reminding parents everywhere that they're already doing better than they think. When she isn't working with animals or writing, she enjoys gardening, reading mysteries and folklore, and exploring the outdoors.

JENNIFER MILLS

(ILLUSTRATOR, COVER DESIGNER)

Jennifer Mills is a Texas-based illustrator and storyteller who loves bringing personality and emotion to every character she creates. For this book, Jennifer designed each of the animal scenes with a playful, heartfelt style that matches the spirit of the author's writing.

Jennifer is also an author of both adult nonfiction and children's books. Her most recent work, Menopause: The Unfiltered Truth, blends humor, honesty, and empowerment for women navigating midlife. She's passionate about creating books that help people feel seen, understood, and a little less alone.

As the founder of Wild Bloom Publishing, Jennifer partners with authors to bring their stories to life—through design, illustration, branding, and book production. She lives in Texas with her husband and kiddos, and two slightly chaotic dogs who believe they run the house.

24 Animal Parenting Fails That Prove You're NOT a Bad Mom

Karen E. Mueller, DVM

Illustrated by Vikki Jackson

K. Mueller Publishing

OTHER BOOKS BY THE AUTHOR

- Humor & Parenting—Some Things Suck™ Series

Some Moms Suck Way More Than You:
24 Animal Parenting Fails That Prove You're NOT a Bad Mom

- Animal Communication & Behavior—Teach Them to Talk™ Series

Dog Button Training: Teach Your Dog to Talk —
A Practical Guide to Button Communication

Dog Button Training Logbook:
Track Your Dog's Words, Progress, and Milestones — A Companion Journal to Dog Button Training

Teach Your Cat to Talk:
A Practical Guide to Button Training for Cats

Cat Button Training Logbook:
Track Your Cat's Words, Progress, and Milestones — A companion journal to Teach Your Cat to Talk: A Practical Guide to Button Training for Cats

- Cryptozoology & Natural History—Creatures of the World™ Series

Cryptid Creatures of the World:
An Illustrated Guide to Myths, Monsters, and Mysterious Creatures Haunting Six Continents

Criaturas Críptidas del Mundo:
Una Guía Ilustrada de Mitos, Monstruos y Criaturas Misteriosas que Habitan en los Seis Continentes

Cryptids of the World:
Where Legends Meet Reality

Críptidos del Mundo:
Donde las Leyendas se Encuentran con la Realidad

Sasquatch:
Insights into Their Lives and Encounters with Humans

BEFORE YOU GO

If Some Dads Suck Way More Than You
gave you a laugh, a little relief,
or a reminder that you're doing a great job—
I'd be grateful if you'd share a great review on Amazon.

Your words help other dads feel seen,
supported, and a little less alone—
and they help this indie author keep writing
the kind of stories that lift people up.

ASIN: 1971218006

Or visit:
Amazon Review Page – Some Dads Suck Way More Than You

Thank you for supporting indie books,
honest humor, and the dads who keep showing up

With gratitude and a smile,
Karen E. Mueller, DVM

References

1. Forsgren, E. (1997). Male–male competition and reproductive success in the sand goby. Animal Behaviour, 54(3), 457–464. https://doi.org/10.1006/anbe.1996.0439.

2. Smith, R. L. (1997). Evolution of paternal care in the giant water bugs (Heteroptera: Belostomatidae). In J. C. Choe & B. J. Crespi (Eds.), The evolution of social behavior in insects and arachnids (pp. 116–149). Cambridge University Press. https://doi.org/10.1017/CBO9780511721953.008

3. Sato, T. (1986). A brood parasitic catfish of mouthbrooding cichlid fishes in Lake Tanganyika. Nature, 323(6086), 58–59. https://doi.org/10.1038/323058a0

4. Crump, M. L. (2002). Natural history of Darwin's frog, Rhinoderma darwinii. Herpetological Natural History, 9(1), 21–30.

5. Gowaty, P. A., & Bridges, W. C. (1991). Nestbox availability affects extra-pair fertilizations and conspecific nest parasitism in eastern bluebirds, Sialia sialis. Animal Behaviour, 41(4), 661–675. https://doi.org/10.1016/S0003-3472(05)80907-7

6. Davies, N. B. (2000). Cuckoos, cowbirds and other cheats. T. & A. D. Poyser.

7. Okuda, N. (2001). The costs of reproduction to males and females of a paternal mouthbrooding cardinalfish. Journal of Fish Biology, 58(3), 776–787. https://doi.org/10.1111/j.1095-8649.2001.tb00534.x

References

8. Jones, A. G., Rosenqvist, G., Berglund, A., Arnold, S. J., & Avise, J. C. (2000). The Bateman gradient and the cause of sexual selection in a sex-role-reversed pipefish. Proceedings of the Royal Society B: Biological Sciences, 267(1448), 677–680. https://doi.org/10.1098/rspb.2000.1055

9. Schwagmeyer, P. L., & Mock, D. W. (2008). Parental provisioning and offspring fitness: Size matters. Animal Behaviour, 75(1), 291–298. https://doi.org/10.1016/j.anbehav.2007.04.020

10. Bradley, R. A. (2013). Common Spiders of North America. University of California Press.

11. Duellman, W. E., & Trueb, L. (1994). Biology of Amphibians. Johns Hopkins University Press.

12. Fernández, G. J., & Reboreda, J. C. (2003). Male parental care in greater rheas (Rhea americana): Collision of investment and mating opportunity. The Auk, 120(2), 486–490. https://doi.org/10.1642/0004-8038(2003)120[0486:MPCRRA]2.0.CO;2

13. Martin, R. W., & Handasyde, K. A. (1999). The koala: Natural history, conservation and management. Krieger Publishing Company.

14. Maxwell, M. R. (1999). Mating behavior. In F. R. Prete, H. Wells, P. H. Wells, & L. E. Hurd (Eds.), The praying mantids (pp. 69–89). Johns Hopkins University Press.

References

15. Neff, B. D., Fu, P., & Gross, M. R. (2003). Sperm investment and alternative mating tactics in bluegill sunfish (Lepomis macrochirus). Behavioral Ecology, 14(5), 634–641. https://doi.org/10.1093/beheco/arg032

16. Auffenberg, W. (1981). The Behavioral Ecology of the Komodo Monitor. University Presses of Florida.

17. Newton, I. (1979). Population Ecology of Raptors. Poyser.

18. Drummond, H., & Osorno, J. L. (1992). Provisioning of nestlings by Magnificent Frigatebirds and Red-footed Boobies on Isla Isabel, Nayarit, Mexico. The Condor, 94(3), 760–765. https://doi.org/10.2307/1369267

19. Amey, A. P., & Whittier, J. M. (2000). Reproductive biology and steroid hormone cycles in the bearded dragon lizard (Pogona barbata) in southeastern Queensland, Australia. General and Comparative Endocrinology, 117(3), 335–342. https://doi.org/10.1006/gcen.1999.7415

20. Sunquist, M. E., & Sunquist, F. (2002). Wild Cats of the World. University of Chicago Press.

www.ingramcontent.com/pod-product-compliance
Lightning Source LLC
Chambersburg PA
CBHW051414050726
47595CB00010B/4069

9781971218007